God is the God of Second Chances

Glennon Jeffries

GOD IS THE GOD OF SECOND CHANCES

BY
GLENNON JEFFRIES

Glennon Jeffries

God is the God of Second Chances
Glennon Jeffries

Published By Parables
November, 2020

All Rights Reserved. No part of this book may be reproduced or utilized in any form or by any means, electronic or mechanical, including photocopying, recording, or by any information storage and retrieval system, without permission in writing from the author.

ISBN 978-1-951497-99-6
Printed in the United States of America

Readers should be aware that Internet Web sites offered as citations and/or sources for further information may have been changed or disappeared between the time this was written and the time it is read.

GOD IS THE GOD OF SECOND CHANCES

BY
GLENNON JEFFRIES

Glennon Jeffries

Chapter 1 – God Created You

God created you in His own image. God knew you before you were born.

Psalm 139:13. You made all the delicate, inner parts of my body and knit me together, in my mother's womb.

Jeremiah 1:5. I knew you before I formed you in your mother's womb.

Ecclesiastes 8:8. None of us has the power to prevent the day of our death.

Job 14:5. You have decided on the length of our lives, and we are not given a minute longer.

All the money in the world can't buy you one second more of time. Before you were born, God knew the exact time you would die.

If you were dying and only had one week to live, what would you ask God for? More time? Or, would you be ready to face judgment? Do you know where you're going when you die? Everything you do in life, from the cradle to the grave, is written in the Lamb's Book of Life.

God loves those whose lives were cut short because of alcohol, drugs, opioids, wars, gun violence, suicide, abortion, and so on. Even though their lives were cut short before their time, God still loves them, just as much as he loves you and me.

God's forgiveness of our sins is much greater than all the stars that are in the entire universe, and greater than all the grains of sand that are here on earth. As far from us as the east is from the west, that's how much God loves you and forgives you. The very first time you ask God to forgive you, you are forgiven. That's how much God loves you. God even loved you before you were born. God's love for you is eternal. God's love for you is agape love.

God created you out of love. God gives you free will to love him or not. God will always love you no matter what you do in life. God's love for you is agape love – unearned, underserved, and unconditional. That's how much he loves you.

God's greatest love for you is the sacrifice of his one and only son Jesus. That's God's agape love. God loved you so much that he nailed all your sins on his son's cross. That's God's agape love. Even when you commit the same sin over and over, God still loves you. That's God's agape love. God even loves those who haven't accepted His son Jesus into their heart yet. That's God's agape love. God will wait patiently for you to make your decision, but time is running out! Nobody is promised tomorrow. You don't know from one minute to the next what's going to happen to you. You don't know when you will breathe your last breath. If you wait until then, it will be too late.

God is a merciful God and loving God. Don't be scared of God. He loves you so much that he sent His son Jesus to die on the cross for your sins. That same Jesus that was on the cross is now in heaven pleading for your sins before His father. That's God's agape love.

God will never stop loving you. Even when you relapse into alcohol, drugs, or any other additions, God still loves you. That's God's agape love that He has for you.

For some, addiction is a very hard habit to break. For others, it's a lifelong battle, but God still loves them. That's God's agape love. We are human and weak. We very easily fall into temptations that lurk around every corner. We were born into sin and we all are going to die a sinner. Nobody's perfect.

Accept Jesus. Jesus is the Way, the Truth, and the Life.

Remember…

Romans 8:38-39. I am convinced that nothing can ever separate us from God's love. Neither death nor life, neither angel nor demons, neither our fears for today nor our worries about tomorrow. Not even the power of hell can separate us from God's love. No power in the sky above or in the earth below – indeed, nothing in all creation will ever be able to separate from the love of God that is revealed in Christ Jesus our Lord.

Romans 3:25. God presented Jesus as a sacrifice for our sins. People are made right with God when they believe that Jesus sacrificed his life.

Psalm 91:4&11. He will cover you with his feathers. For He will order his angels to protect you wherever you go.

Psalm 51:4. Against you, and you alone, have I sinned; I have done what is evil in your sight.

1 Peter 2:24. He personally carried our sins in his body on the cross so that we can be dead to sin. By his wounds, you are healed.

Colossians 2:14. He canceled the record of the charges against us and took it away by nailing it to the cross.

Jesus is the way the truth and the life.

God is the God of Second Chances.

Glennon Jeffries

Chapter 2 – Free Will

Did Adam and Eve have free will after they sinned in the Garden of Eden? Yes!

Everything God creates is perfect. The stars and galaxies throughout the universe, the positioning and rotation of the planets, the distance from the sun to the earth, and the only planet in the entire solar system that can sustain life...God's intelligent design is perfect in every way.

God even created the perfect man and woman: Adam and Eve. God made them perfect in every way because God Himself is perfect. Until Satan, the serpent came along and caused Eve to sin and fall from grace. Then Eve caused Adam to sin and fall from grace. So they both sinned and were not perfect in God's sight anymore. That's why they will never again return to that perfect place in the Garden of Eden. That's why God stationed a mighty cherubim and placed a flaming sword to guard the way to the Tree of Life.

Because Adam and Eve fell from grace and were not perfect in God's sight anymore, they both were banished from the Garden of Eden. God gave Adam and Eve free will, and then they sinned and were not perfect anymore in God's sight. Because God Himself is perfect, and everything God creates is perfect, God made Adam and Eve intelligent enough to know right from wrong.

When Adam and Eve sinned, sin and death entered the world. That's when free will started. None of us will ever be perfect in God's sight, because we all sin and fall short of the glory of God. In the beginning, God existed. He is all-knowing and all-loving!

And God will always be perfect and God will always love you no matter what sins you have committed.

Even God's chosen people had free will to do good or evil, to worship God or worship false gods or idols, or to commit sexual sin and adultery. Even after all the signs and wonders that God performed in Egypt through Moses and the parting of the sea, God's chosen people were still sinning. They even built and worshiped a golden calf while God was giving Moses the 10 commandments. Even after all the moaning and complaining they did from the time they left Egypt to Mount Sinai, and even after all they did, God still loved his chosen people. God loves you just as much.

Even God's prophets and kings had free will. The Lord sent his prophets to warn His kings when they did wrong and those who went against God's commands. King David committed adultery with Bathsheba and got her pregnant and had her husband killed in battle so he could cover up what he did. Then he married her. They had a son and they named him Solomon. King David asked God for forgiveness for what he did and God forgave him. After the death of King David, Solomon became king and was the wisest person to ever live. People came from near and far to seek Solomon's wisdom. Solomon became the richest man to ever live.

When Jesus was born, God even gave Him free will, just like you and me. And while Jesus was living here on earth, He had the same kind of temptations that you and I have. We failed, but Jesus didn't fail. When Jesus was born, He was born perfect and without sin. But when Jesus died, He died the worst of all sinners. By Jesus' suffering and death on the cross, He defeated the devil by nailing all your sins on His cross. And by His resurrection, He has set us free! Now that Jesus has ascended into heaven, He sits at God's right-hand pleading for all our sins. That's how much God loves you. God did that for you and me.

God's love for you is agape love – unearned, underserved, and unconditional. God even gives those not born yet free will. If God did not give us free will, then we all would be like robots.

God gives you free will to do good or evil. So it's your choice – heaven or hell.
Remember how Satan was thrown to earth before the creation of man? Satan is still here today seeking your soul to ruin.

God gives you free will to do good.

Seek the Lord while He may be found, because nobody is promised tomorrow. Fill your heart with God's Holy Word – for all scripture is given by the inspiration of God to forgive one another as God forgave you. Forgive one another seventy times seven. Love one another as the Lord loves you – even those who hate you.

Peter the apostle, Paul the evangelist, and Billy Graham led tens of millions to the Lord. Mother Teresa saved hundreds of thousands from starvation in the streets of Calcutta. Pope John Paul II was filled with the Holy Spirit. He led tens of thousands of youth to the Lord. They did well with free will.

God gives you free will to do evil.

Killing another human being, committing adultery, looking at porn, using the Lord's name in vain, embezzlement, extortion, stealing, robbery, lying, and so on are all evil.
Over the centuries, some countries used religion to invade other countries. Some countries invaded other countries to expand their influence and power. If God wanted to, He could send down one angel from heaven to destroy all the nations on earth.

God is a loving God and a forgiving God.

No one is righteous, not even one. You don't know from one minute to the next what's

Going to happen to you. Once you breathe your last breath, it will be too late to repent. Accept Jesus into your heart as your Lord and Savior. Nobody is guaranteed tomorrow. Jesus is the Way, the Truth, and the Life.

God is the God of Second Chances.

Chapter 3 – Free Will to be Born Again

God gives you free will to be born again.

Ephesians 2:5. It is only by God's grace that you have been saved.

John 3:3. Jesus replied "I tell you the truth, unless you are born again, you cannot see the kingdom of God."

Nicodemus was the first to be born again, two thousand years ago, when he saw Jesus in the garden at night. Two thousand years later Jesus gives you the opportunity to be born again.

To be born again, all you have to do is ask God to send you His Holy Spirit to guide you through His Holy Scriptures, and believe what it says. Repent of your sins. Say the sinner's prayer. Accept Jesus into your heart as your Lord and Savior and then you will be born again.

Ask Jesus to send his Holy Spirit to help you walk down that narrow road that leads to your eternal reward. Even though you are born again, you will sin and die a sinner. God's love and mercy are much greater than any sin that you will ever commit in your life. Jesus was scourged with a cat o'nine tails. He suffered for our sins all the way to the cross and died a horrible death. But on the third day, Jesus resurrected from the dead, and He will never again die. From this day on, He will sit in a place of honor at God's right hand pleading for our sins. He did that for you and me.

Ephesians 3:17. Christ will make His home in your heart as you trust in him.

John 5:29. Those who have done good will rise to experience eternal life.

1 John 5:1. Everyone who believes that Jesus is the Christ has become a child of God.

1 John 4:9. God showed how much He loved us by sending His one and only Son into the world so that we might have eternal life.

Romans 10:9. If you confess with your mouth that Jesus is Lord and believe in your heart that God raised Him from the dead, you will be saved.

Romans 8:11. The Spirit of God, who raised Jesus from the dead, lives in you.

John 3:14 - 15. The Son of Man must be lifted up so that everyone who believes in Him will have eternal life.

Revelation 3:20. Look! I stand at the door and knock. If you hear My voice and open the door, I will come in.

Being born again is not a one-time event, but a lifelong process, a journey of transformation and renewing of your mind through God's Holy Word.

Ephesians 2:8. God saved you by grace when you believe.

1 Peter 1:3. It is by His great mercy that we have been born again because God raised Jesus Christ from the dead.

The Sinner's Prayer

Jesus, Son of the Living God, have mercy on me, a sinner. I repent of my sins. Jesus come into my heart as my Lord and Savior. I truly believe that You are the Son of the Living God. I truly believe that You suffered for my sins, died, and resurrected, and are now in heaven at God's right-hand pleading for our sins. Amen.

Being born again is God's greatest free gift He gives you. Salvation is a promise, not a feeling. It's a free gift. God gives you free will to be born again. Only you can make that decision – no one else. Repent, accept Jesus into your heart as your Lord and Savior. No matter what decision you make, God will always love you. God will wait patiently for you. But nobody is promised tomorrow.

Now that you made the right decision to be born again, you are on your way to heaven to live with Jesus Christ our Lord forever.

Jesus is the Way, the Truth, and the Life.

Now that you are born again, start reading the Bible. Read the Gospel of John.

God is the God of Second Chances.

Glennon Jeffries

Chapter 4 – Intelligent Design

God's intelligent design, all around us seen, and unseen.

Genesis 1:27. God created human beings in his own image. In the image of God, He created them. Male and female, He created them.

Psalm 139:13. You made all the delicate, inner parts of my body and knit me together in my mother's womb.

God has his imprint inside each one of us. It's laminin, a protein network, the foundation for most cells and organs. It holds the ligaments together. And best of all, when you look inside each laminin cell, each cell has the shape of a cross – a reminder of God's sacrifice of His one and only Son Jesus.

Only God can create such a complex human body.

The main central nervous system, composed of the brain and spinal cord, has several major parts. These include the peripheral nervous system, sensory system, glial cells, neurons, action potential, synapses, neurotransmitters, neurotransmitter receptors, and more.

Humans have five vital organs that are essential for survival: the brain, heart, lungs, stomach, and kidneys.

Brain. The brain is the central controller for the human body. The brain is a part of the nervous system. The brain keeps the heart pumping blood.

Heart. The heart is part of the cardiovascular system and is responsible for bringing blood to the various tissues in the body. The blood carries oxygen and white blood cells, which is a part of the immune system.

Lungs. The lungs are the major organ that provides oxygen exchange. The lungs contain tiny bronchial alveoli that help the body eliminate carbon dioxide.

Stomach. The stomach is a major organ that holds food and sends it to the intestines for digestion and absorption. The pancreas and the gallbladder provide enzymes that break down the stomach content.

Kidneys. The kidneys are a part of the endocrine system. These organs provide the filtration system necessary for metabolic waste in tissue.

Anatomy of the body. The body has several systems. These include the digestive system, endocrine system, immune system, lymphatic system, nervous system, muscular system, reproductive system, skeletal system, respiratory system, urinary system, and integumentary system.

There are 25 trillion red cells in the human body. There's an average of 7,000 white blood cells per microliter of blood. If you could take out all the blood vessels inside an adult, it would stretch 100,000 miles. The blood vessels of an average child would stretch 60,000 miles.

There are 60,000 miles of blood vessels through which the heart pumps blood. The average body makes about two to three million red blood cells every second from 173 to 259 billion red cells a day.

There are 37.2 trillion cells, 600 muscles, and 206 bones in the human body.

God is the God of Second Chances

The human eye is one of God's complex creations. The retina contains millions of tiny light-sensing nerve cells called rods and cones. There are seven other important parts of the eye. These include tears, cornea, pupil, iris, lens, retina and sclera. They each have an important function.

After seeing the complex creation of the human body, I believe there is a God. Only God can create such a marvelous thing.

In the beginning, God created heaven, earth, and man, all in seven days. This includes the trillions of galaxies and stars that are in the vast universe and that is still expanding today. This equals infinity. It would take infinity for any of Darwin's theories to be proven.

God even created things you can't see. You can't see the air you breathe, yet it keeps you alive. You can't see the wind blowing or where it's going, yet you can feel it. God created things you can see, and things you can't see.

Genesis 1:1. In the beginning, God created the heavens and the earth.

Genesis 2:1-2. The creation of heaven and earth and everything in them was completed. On the seventh day, God finished his work of creation.

The night sky is God's masterpiece where there are over one billion trillion stars in that vast universe. The Hubble space telescope can see close to two billion galaxies. Some galaxies have billions of stars, and others have trillions of stars. The Hubble Space telescope can see from 10 to 15 billion light-years away!

The Universe is still expanding, which means there are tens of billions of galaxies and tens of trillions of stars that are beyond the Hubble Telescope. That equals infinity, which is bigger than the googolplex (10^{100} zeros).

Psalm 19:1. The heavens proclaim the glory of God. The skies display his craftsmanship.

The earth is the only planet that is fine-tuned for humans to live on and survive. The oxygen level has to be 21% to sustain life – not 21.5 percent, and not 20.5 percent. God knew what he was doing.

Water on earth is 97% saltwater and 3% freshwater.

The sun is 9,941 degrees Fahrenheit.

The distance from the sun to the earth is 93 million miles – just the right amount of distance to sustain life here on earth. If the sun was 92 million miles away from earth, it would be over 1,000 degrees Fahrenheit on earth. If the sun was 94 million miles away from earth, it would be over 1,000 degrees Fahrenheit below zero or more on earth. We would not exist here on earth today. God sure knew what he was doing when he created the earth. It is the only planet that humans can live on.

The planet earth that we live on spins on its axis at 1,000 miles per hour. Are you dizzy yet?

Distance from the Planets to Earth			
Millions of Miles		Billions of Miles	
Mercury	56.9	Uranus	1.69
Venus	25.7	Neptune	2.70
Mars	48.6	Pluto (dwarf)	3.15
Jupiter	390.6		
Saturn	792.2		

The distance of every other planet in our solar system to the sun will never ever be able to sustain any kind of life. Even in the beginning when God created the universe, none of these planets were able to sustain life. The earth is the only planet that God created to sustain life. Even if the universe is still here a billion

God is the God of Second Chances

years from now, these planets will never be able to sustain life. God sure knew what he was doing when he created the universe.

Some galaxies have billions of stars and some have trillions of stars. Our Milky Way has two billion stars and is over 100,000 light-years wide. The Whirlpool galaxy has 100 billion stars. The Andromeda Galaxy and Messier 87 each have one trillion stars! IC 1101 has 100 trillion stars!

I have more faith in God's intelligent design of the creation of the human body and the vast endless universe than I do in any of Darwin's theories. Darwin was born in the 1800s. But God was never born – nobody created God. He existed before time. As time went on, God created man. None of Darwin's theories were ever proven to be right – seen or unseen.

The Amazon rainforest is the home to over 30 million species of amphibians, birds and insects. There are documentaries on insects, amphibians, birds, animals, and reptiles. See how God created them with the instinct to live and survive, from birth to death?

There are over 3.5 trillion fish in all the oceans. The deepest part of the ocean is the Marian trenches, which are 26,000 feet deep and have fish that deep and on the ocean floor.

God's magnificent beauty is everywhere – coral reefs, the Seven Wonders of the World, the Grand Canyon, Yellowstone National Park, the Great Smoky Mountains, Olympia State Park, and other national parks. You can see God's beauty while hiking on trails in the forest, hiking to waterfalls, going into the rainforest, and on other nature trails. God's creation of the earth is beautiful – it's just a glance of what heaven looks like.

Well-Known Atheists Who Converted to Christianity

Well-known atheists turned Christian include Albert Einstein, Isaac Newton, Galileo, Francis S. Collins, C.S. Lewis, Lee Strobel and others.

God's intelligent design is everywhere, seen and unseen. You be the judge.
Do you believe in God's intelligent design or do you believe in Darwin's theory? It's your choice. Your eternity, heaven or hell, depends on your decision.

God's intelligent design surpassed anything that any human will ever create.

God is the God of Second Chances.

Chapter 5 – Robert, the Greatest Quarterback Ever

Robert played quarterback all throughout junior high school. Robert lost only one game. Robert broke nine junior high records as a quarterback and received all kinds of awards as a quarterback.

When Robert was in his last year of junior high, he met a girl. She led him to the Lord. Robert started going to the youth group at her church, and he started reading the Bible. Robert could not wait to go back to the youth group. He loved the youth group so much that he was thinking about quitting football to concentrate on being a minister. When he told his coach what he wanted to do, the coach told Robert to go and talk to the minister of the youth group so he could tell him what to do. The coach told Robert, "I hope you will continue playing football because you are one of the best junior high players ever to play football." Robert told the coach, "You will be the first to know." So, Robert left to go and see the minister.

When Robert got there knocked on the door, a voice on the other side said to come in. Robert opened the door and said, "Hello, my name is Robert."

The minister said, "I know who you are. You are one of the best junior high quarterbacks ever. My name is Peter, what's on your mind?"

Robert replied, "I feel like I have a calling to be a minister."

Peter asked, "How do you know?"

He said, "I have a burning feeling inside of me every time I read the Bible, and when I play football I have the same feeling. I don't know what to do."

Peter told Robert, "You have a calling to be a minister. I am looking for someone to be in charge of the youth group, would you be interested?"

Robert said, "Yes, I will be glad to."

Peter replied, "You will start in three weeks. The person that's in charge is leaving us to be a minister." He then said, "Don't quit football, and if you have the same feeling when you finish high school, then you have a calling to be a minister. That means you can go to a college where you can study to be a minister and play football at the same time."

Robert then said, "Thank you, Mr. Peter, for the advice on what to do and for letting me be in charge of the youth group. Thank you."

Robert played quarterback in junior high from 2013-2015. His record was 26-1. Robert's only loss was in his very first game he started. In that game, he was injured in the first quarter and remained out of the game as a precaution. They were trailing by seven points, and lost by seven points. Robert only lost a game in junior high.

Robert started off high school football where he left off in junior high. Robert has been undefeated in high school from 2016 to 2019 at Newman High, where they have been state champions for the past three years, and if Newman wins this Saturday, they will be state champions again for the fourth year in a row. It will be the first time in history that a team has won four state titles in a row. Newman has been nationally ranked for four years in a row. The first year they were ranked number five, and the last three years ranked the number one team in the nation.

Robert is undefeated as the quarterback, with a record of 47-0. Robert refuses to take credit for the success of the team. He says winning is a team effort. Robert broke ten high school records in the nation and received dozens of awards nationally. If Robert wins this Saturday's game, he will be the state and national MVP

God is the God of Second Chances

for 4 years. Robert will become the first player to ever win four MVP awards in a row.

Before each game, Robert would get down on one knee and say a prayer. Now, he has the whole team praying before each game; he even has players from the other teams on one knee praying with them. Robert is also in charge of the youth group, where they praise and worship every Wednesday night.

Now there's a new kid on the block. It's St. Augustine High's quarterback who is undefeated, with a record of 11-0. Some say their quarterback is just as good as Robert. Some say he's even better.

Robert is a very likable guy. He prays for the opposing team before each game. He even prayed for St. Augustin's quarterback, wishing him well and the best of luck in Saturday's game. Robert and St. Augustine's quarterback are neck and neck for the MVP award. Robert welcomes the competition. St. Augustine is number two in the state and number five in the nation. The game of the year is this Saturday and that's all everybody has been talking about all week. Both teams have won their first playoff game and there will be recruiters at the game from colleges and universities across the country to see Robert play. The recruiters are from LSU; Alabama; Clemson; Ohio State; Florida; Arkansas State, which is a long shot; plus 15 other colleges and universities. They all want Robert to play at their school, but Robert might be going to a Christian college that has a football team, in case he still has a calling to be a minister.

Both teams have been practicing for Saturday's big game, which is three days away.
Every night during football season, Robert would go home and study his next week's opponent and his team's game plan. This is the biggest game of his career.

After practice, some of the players were going to the mall, they asked Robert to go with them to celebrate another undefeated season. Robert said "Ok, I will go on one condition: if you get me home early enough to study Saturday's game plans."

The team agreed. They left for the mall around 7:25. They got in their car and turned right onto a one-way street going the speed limit. There was a car coming down the wrong way of the same street at a high rate of speed. They could not get out the way in time and the next thing you know, the car hit them head-on and the force of the impact caused their car to flip over twice.

There was a lawyer named Jake who worked at a prestigious law firm. Jake had just won his biggest case ever for the firm and received a big sizable bonus for his efforts.

Jake, the Lawyer

Jake is a heavy drinker. When Jake gets home from work, he drinks 10 to 12 bottles of beer every night. The lawyers at the law firm told Jake he needs to get help with his drinking problem.

Jake told them "I do not have any drinking problem, and I do not need any help at all."

Jake has had 2 DWIs in the past. Jake is really good friends with two judges. Jake goes to lunch with the judges two to three times a week, and sometimes he will buy them a drink. The two judges who are friends with Jake expunged the two DWIs and in turn, Jake donates money to their campaigns. Jake now only drinks at his house since he has had two DWIs.

Jake received his bonus today. Instead of going home to celebrate, he decided to go to a bar, which will be the first time in three years. After Jake got his second DWI, he promised the two judges he's friends with and the lawyers at his law firm that he would only drink at home. But tonight was very special for Jake. He received his big bonus and wanted to go out to celebrate at a bar instead of going home. So, he went to a bar where nobody would recognize him. When Jake walked into the bar at around 6 p.m., he sat down in the corner on a stool and started drinking. Then he started buying rounds for everybody in the bar.

After Jake had 12 beers, the bartender refused to sell Jake any more beer. Jake was so mad that he staggered out the door to his car. It was around 7:20 p.m. Nobody had ever seen Jake in the bar before. The name of the bar was The One-Way Bar, because it's on a one-way street.

When Jake got in his car, he turned the wrong way down the one-way street. He was going at a high rate of speed. As he was going down the street, he sideswiped six to seven cars then he hit another car head-on, causing it to flip over twice. The occupants of the car that was hit were wearing their seat belts, but the force of the impact caused some of the occupants to be in critical to serious condition. You could hear them moaning in pain. Debris was scattered over 50 feet. Nobody knew that the occupants of the car were Newman high football players and that one of them was Robert. The driver who caused the accident didn't have a scratch on him.

The four ambulances that rushed to the scene were there within minutes. A crowd gathered around the scene of the accident. They were coming from blocks away when they heard the crash. When the paramedics arrived, they were able to take three of the injured from the car. The fourth passenger was Robert, who was pinned in the front seat of the car. The front part of the car was against Robert's right leg.

The paramedics put the others on stretchers and took them to the hospital. They looked to be in critical condition. They finally got the front passengers from the car. Someone in the crowd said, "Hey, he looks like Robert, the Newman High quarterback."

Robert got the worst of it. They put a brace on his neck and his right leg was bleeding. They rushed him to the hospital.

When Robert was pinned in the car, he promised God that if he let me live, he would forgive the man that hit them. The ambulances dropped off the injured and rushed them to the trauma center. They were running all kinds of tests on them.

The news media got wind that one of the injured might be Robert and three other Newman players and arrived outside the hospital. The hospital notified their families. Fifteen minutes later, their parents started arriving at the hospital. The news media noticed that one of the parents looks like Robert's parents. Fifteen minutes later, a hospital spokesman came out and told the media that they would have a news conference tomorrow at 11:00 a.m. and would give an update on the condition of the injured.

As the spokesman was turning around to go back in, a reporter yelled out, "Is one of the injured Robert?

The spokesman said, "No comment," and went in.

When the reporters turned around, they noticed a man walking into the emergency room. One of the reporters said, "He looks like Coach Martin. If that's him, it must be Robert and three other players that were in the accident. Why else would Coach Martin be here?"

The reporters left for the night. The next morning the reporters would be at the courthouse at 10:00 a.m. and then at the hospital at 11 a.m. for the update.

When the police arrived at the scene, they did a breathalyzer test on the driver of the other car. He was three times over the legal limit. He was so impaired he didn't even know he was in an accident. They took him to jail where they fingerprinted him and took a mug shot. The next morning, they would go before a judge around 10:00 a.m. to decide if he could post bail.

They tried not to let the mug shot get out, but someone in the police department found out that the front passenger in the car was

God is the God of Second Chances

Robert and sent the mug shot to all the news media outlets. The media posted the mug shot all over the news. The mug shot was Jake Peterson, a lawyer who works for the prestigious law firm called Andrey and Son's Law Firm. They learned that Jake had two prior DWIs. Jake's mugshot made him look like a homeless person on the street.

The next morning, the news media gathered outside at the courthouse to see if the person that caused the accident would post bail or stay in jail until his trial. They learned that he would be representing himself. The two judges that Jake knows recused themselves from the case because of a conflict of interest. They have been the best of friends with Jake for years. The case was assigned to another judge, who denied bail for Jake and decided that Jake should remain in jail till his trial. The judge said he could revisit his decision at a later date.

At 10:40 a.m., the media rushed from the courthouse to the hospital for the latest update. The spokesperson for the hospital came out and said that at 7:35 p.m. last night, there was a car accident and there were rumors that four Newman high football players were involved in the accident. He confirmed the rumors were true and that Robert was one of the ones in the car. He said that Robert is in serious condition with a sprained shoulder and that his right knee was crushed from being pinned against the motor.

The spokesperson then said, "I hate to be the one to tell you this, but Robert will never play football again because of the severity of his injury. Robert will walk with a limp for the rest of his life – his football career is over."

Robert was devastated when he heard the news. Robert was the greatest quarterback ever to play football. His records will be hard to break for years to come.

Coach Martin arrived at the hospital right after the accident happened and stayed overnight at the hospital with Robert's family. He broke down and cried when he saw the condition Robert was in. When Robert woke up, he was alert and in little pain. He was able to talk to his family and coach Martin. Robert asked his coach to write a letter to the judge and Jake's lawyer. When Robert finished the letters, he asked the coach to give one to each of them and the coach said okay.

Coach Martin left the hospital at 11:00 a.m. and Robert's family left at 3:00 p.m. Later that evening, St. Augustine's quarterback went to see Robert around 5 p.m. He had heard that Robert will never play football again. They visited for over two hours. Robert told St. Augustine's quarterback, whose name is Sammy, that he was so angry at the man that hit him, even after he told God that he would forgive the man that hit them.

He said "I broke my promise and asked God to forgive me for being so angry at the man and for what I said. I told God I was sorry."

Robert and Sammy know each other well. They go to the same prayer meeting. Sammy is in the music ministry at the praise and worship service. Sammy told Robert that he would keep him in his prayers. Robert then told Sammy that the recruiters were here to see him play but he can't play anymore.

Robert then said "Remember this: four years from now, these same recruiters will be back here to see you play. I hope it's you that breaks my records."

Robert then told Sammy, "Thank you for coming."

Sammy left. On his way out, the reporters noticed him. They ran up to him and asked "Why are you here? Is everything alright?"

Sammy said "Yes, I just went to see a friend."

One of the reporters asked him, "Is it Robert."

Sammy replied, "Yes, we are good friends."

They asked him how Robert was doing. Sammy said "He's devastated because he will never play football again. He knew it the moment of the accident."

It is well known that Jake has a drinking problem and that he refused to get help. None of the lawyers at his law firm would represent him. Jake decided he would not represent himself at his trial. He decided to get a lawyer from another law firm to handle his case.

Jake's lawyer decided to talk to the judge to see if Jake could serve the remainder of his time at home till his trial, so on Friday morning, Jake's lawyer went to see the judge. He asked the judge if Jake surrendered his passport and wore an ankle monitor, could he be tested once a week. The judge said he would agree on one condition: if Jake would be tested four times a week, not once a week. Jake's lawyer agreed to these terms, so Jake went home under house arrest until his trial.

Coach Martin called Robert to tell him that he gave the letters to Judge Walter and Jake's lawyer and that he and the other coach were going to get together tonight to say the game would go on as scheduled.

Robert said "All four of us would want the game to go on. There will be recruiters at the game. The game sold out and tickets are hard to find."

Robert then told the coach, "I could see my life flash before my eyes when l was in the car. I promised God that if he let me live, I would forgive the man that hit us. Since I can't play football anymore, I will study to be a minister because I still have a burning feeling in my heart every time I read the Bible. I believe God is calling me to be a minister instead of playing football."

Robert's Letter to the Judge

I am writing this letter to the presiding judge.

Dear Judge Walter, my name is Robert. I am the quarterback for Newman High School.

Even though I will never be able to play football again, I forgive Mr. Jake for causing me to never play football again. I pray and ask you to please give Mr. Jake a light sentence if he agrees to go to AA for help. Mr. Jake could be somebody's father, brother, son, uncle, or grandpa. Please take my request under consideration. Please give Mr. Jake a second chance at life. God is the God of the second chances. I forgive Mr. Jake.

Sincerely yours,
Robert Hamilton.

The Judge's Response

I am writing this letter to Robert in response to his letter.

Dear Robert,

I received your letter today from Coach Martin. I read it, it was a heartfelt letter. I will take what you wrote under consideration when I hand down my sentence.
Jake had two prior DWIs. If Mr. Jake shows me that he has remorse for what he did and will go to AA meetings, then I will take your requests under consideration.

Sincerely yours,
Judge Walter

P.S. Robert, God gave you the gift of forgiveness.

God is the God of Second Chances

Robert's Letter to Jake

I am writing this letter to Mr. Jake.

Mr. Jake,

I want to let you know that I forgive you. It was very hard for me to do. You took my dream away from me of playing in the NFL in the future. I asked the judge to be lenient in his sentencing you. I believe in second chances. I hope you will get the help you need and go to AA. If you show the judge that you are remorseful and that you are sorry, then he will give you a lighter sentence. What you did to me, you have to live with for the rest of your life. That's punishment enough. I want you to know I forgive you and that God is the God of second chances.

Sincerely yours
Robert Hamilton

Jake's Response to Robert

I am writing this letter to Robert. I received your letter today.

Robert, I am sorry for ruining your football career. No matter what I say or do, you will never play football again because of me. I don't see how you can forgive me. I sure would not forgive the person that ruined my chances of playing in the NFL. Sorry, Robert, I will seek your advice and get the help I need. Words cannot say how sorry I am. Thank you for forgiving me, it means a lot to me. I will never forget the kindness you have shown me. God bless you, Robert.

Sincerely yours
Jake Peterson

Robert called the news media and asked if they would read a letter over the air to the people of Louisiana. They agreed.

Robert's Letter to the People of Louisiana

To the people of Louisiana from Robert, Newman High School's quarterback.

I would like to thank the people of Louisiana for their prayers and well wishes and the love they showed me. Your prayers lifted up my spirit when l needed it the most.

Over the years, you have shown me kindness and made me feel like l was part of your family every Friday night. I would like to thank you for your hospitality over the years. Even though l will never play football again, I forgive the drunk driver that has caused me to never play football again. When l say my prayers, l will ask God that Mr. Jake will get the help he needs with his drinking problem. I forgive Mr. Jake. I hope you can forgive him too. He could be somebody's daddy or brother.

I have opened up a new chapter in my life. I have been offered a free scholarship at Liberty University. From there, I will go to seminary school. l have a calling to be a minister. I have had that feeling inside of me for years. I have moved on with my life. God bless the people of Louisiana.

Love,
Robert Hamilton

P.S. Go Newman!

Saturday night was here – it was supposed to be the biggest game of the year, but now it's just a regular game. Four of Newman's best players will not be in the game because of the accident. Newman's backup quarterback, who has never played a game

God is the God of Second Chances

before, will have his first start. His last game was in junior high. The game is going to be nationally televised. The Newman players decided to dedicate this game to the four players in the accident.

The players for both teams went out in the middle of the field and got on one knee for Robert and the three other players in a moment of silence. Robert knew a lot of St. Augustine players in the youth group, where everybody knows each other. After kneeling, both teams went to their sideline.

St. Augustine won the toss. They received the kickoff. They went down the field to their own 47-yard line and then scored a touchdown within three minutes. The score was 7-0.

Newman received the ball and went to their own 40-yard line.
They went three and out.
They kicked the ball to St. Augustine's 32-yard line. St. Augustine went 30 yards and then punted.

The first-quarter came to an end with St. Augustine up 7-0.

At the start of the second quarter, Newman went down the field and made a 32-yard field goal. The score was now 7-3.

Newman kicked the ball to St. Augustine, but St. Augustine did not score. At half time, the score remained 7-3, with St. Augustine on top.

At the start of the third quarter, Newman received the ball and went down the field and made another field goal. The score was now 7-6.

Now it was St. Augustine's turn to receive the ball. They made a field goal, and now the score was 10-6.

Newman went down the field and made a touchdown with 3:45 left in the game. Newman was up 13-10!

St Augustine went down to Newman's 40-yard line. On 4th down, St. Augustine made a field goal, the longest in the kicker's history. The score was tied at 13-13.

Newman got the ball with 1:45 left in the game. They went down to St. Augustine's 40-yard line. Newman's field goal unit kicked the ball and missed, but there was a flag. Offside St Augustine! Five-yard penalty and now Newman has another chance to kick a 35-yard field goal. St. Augustine called a time out.

Newman kicked the ball and made the field goal. The score was now 16-13. Newman then kicked off to St. Augustine with 56 seconds left. St. Augustine ran the ball to their own 48 with 45 seconds left. St. Augustine's quarterback then threw the ball to Newman's 42-yard line. St Augustine handed the ball off and the player fumbled the ball. A Newman player recovered the ball!

The Newman quarterback took a knee. St. Augustine called time out. Newman ran the ball to the 34-yard line with 27 seconds left. St. Augustine called their last time out. Newman then ran the ball and they ran the clock out.

Newman won the game 16 to 13!

The field goal kicker won the MVP of the game. The state and national both gave MVP to Robert for four years of being undefeated. This was the first time in history for something like this to happen. Newman was number one in the state and in the national polls for three years in a row for the first time ever.

The people were celebrating in the street like it was Mardi Gras.

Robert watched the game on TV with his family. Coach Martin called Robert after the game. He was so excited that he was crying. He was so happy.

God is the God of Second Chances.

Chapter 6 – Spike

God is the God of Second Chances, from Hell and Back

My name is Spike. I have been in a motorcycle gang for 15 years. I've been in and out of jail. I've been stabbed many times. I had been taking drugs for years when I OD'd for the third time. At the time I OD'd, I was so wasted that I fell out of a two-story window and died. I could see my body lying on the ground. I could see gang members around me…and I could see my girlfriend holding me in her arms, crying. I could see my body getting further and further away.

The next thing I knew, I was going through a dark tunnel. I could not see any light. The further I went into the tunnel, the darker it was. When I reached the bottom of the tunnel, it was pitch dark. I could not see a thing. It was so hot my skin was burning. When I looked around, I noticed flames in a far distance. I heard crying and screaming coming from the flames.

I heard voices in the flames saying "Please God, please help me. Please forgive me. Please give me a drop of water! I am sorry! Please get me out of here!" It smelled like sulfur mix with the rottenest, stinkiest garbage you would ever smell.

I said to myself, "I must be in hell." Then I saw three creatures in a distance coming towards me. I could only see their red eyes. They seemed to be about 10 feet tall. I have never been so scared in my life. As the three creatures got closer and closer, they got bigger and bigger. They looked to be 20 feet tall. They were groaning and screeching so loud that it was ear piercing.

There was no way out of here. I had never read the Bible in my whole life. I had never been in a church. I had never prayed in my entire life, I don't even know how to pray, so I said what everybody else here was saying.

I cried out, "Please God, please help me. Please forgive me. I am sorry! Please get me out of here!"

Then I remembered a song that my grandma used to sing to me when I was a little boy. It went like this:

> Jesus loves me this I know
> For the Bible tells me so

I kept saying that song over and over, hoping God would hear me.

Then I told God, "If you get me out of here, I will quit the gang and be a minister for gang members. I will tell other gang members that you, God, are real and that hell is real because I was there and saw it with my own two eyes."

After I said that, the three creatures were six feet away and they reached for me to throw me into the fire. Then I said, "Please, God, give me a second chance!"

The next thing I knew, I was jolted back into my body by the paramedics. They then found a pulse and started an IV drip. I was bleeding so much that they started giving me blood.

God gave me a second chance!

The paramedics rushed me to the hospital. I was in the hospital for eight months. I had a broken back, ribs, hip, and ankle. My girlfriend would not leave my side. The next day, I hardly talked, but I told my girlfriend everything I had seen and heard when I was in hell. She had a scary look on her face, but she believed everything I told her.

While I was in the hospital, I received intense therapy five days a week for eight months. When they released me from the hospital, I was still in pain. I had to do eight more weeks of therapy. I will be walking with a limp for the rest of my life.

When they released me from the hospital, I asked my girlfriend if she would marry me and she said yes. We went to the justice of the peace to get married. My new wife and I went to see the gang. When we got there, everybody was glad to see us. We told them that we had just gotten married. They were not surprised – they said they knew it was going to happen sooner or later.

I told the gang everything that happened, from the time I died and went to hell to the time the paramedics brought me back. I told them everything I heard and saw while I was in hell. Some believed me and some didn't. Out of 185 gang members, 137 believed what I said. I told them that I was quitting the gang and becoming a minister for all the gangs in the area.

God gave me a second chance! I will be going to a Bible school, and when I am finished, I will have a church for gang members.

After we left, we went looking for a Christian book store to buy a Bible. I found a book store two miles away. We got there in 15 minutes. When we walked in, everybody was staring at us because of all the tattoos and piercings we have all over us. They kept on staring.

I went up to the manager and asked, "What is the easiest Bible to read?"

He said in a shaky voice, "The NLT Bible."

I told him, "I never did read a Bible before in my whole life. I want to learn how to read the Bible so I can get to know God and his son Jesus." I then asked him if there were any prayer meetings in the area.

He said, "I don't know of any. I am new in town."

There was a lady in the store and she wasn't even scared to talk to us. She came up to us and introduced herself.

She said, "Hello, my name is Grace."

I said, "I'm Spike. This my wife, Darlene."

Grace started telling us about her church. She invited us to go the following Sunday. She told us her dad is the pastor and that they have praise and worship services every Wednesday night, where people give their testimony. I told her everything about my past. I even told her about me going to hell. I then told her I would like to be a minister and open up a church for gang members.

Before we left, Grace gave us some Bible verses to look up and gave us her number in case we had questions or didn't understand something. I thanked her for everything. On our way out, she gave us the address of her church. I told her we would be there.

Sunday came and we went to her church. When we walked in, she was in the back of the church. She told us she was glad we could come. Her dad was in the back greeting everyone. When he saw Grace, he walked over and she introduced us to him.

She said, "Dad, this is Spike and his wife Darlene. We met at the bookstore."

Her dad said, "Glad to meet you. My name is Josh. Grace has told me everything about you."

Josh then told me, "You have a powerful testimony that can help thousands of kids in the youth group and high school, their friends and family, and even church members. Will you give your testimony this Wednesday?"

I said "Sure, I would be glad to!"

God is the God of Second Chances

After the service was over, Josh asked everybody to please be seated. He said, "This Wednesday night, I have a very special guest. His name is Spike. Spike used to be in a motorcycle gang. He is going to give his testimony about how he died and went to hell and how when he asked God to give him a second chance, He did!

Josh then asked if I would come out and say something. When I was walking out, everybody was shocked to see how I looked. They could not stop staring at me because I had tattoos and piercings all over.

The minister gave me the microphone and I said in a raspy voice, "My name is Spike. I am here to tell you there is a hell and it is real! I know, because I was there and I saw it with my own two eyes. Comes this Wednesday to hear the truth about hell. Bring your family and friends! See you Wednesday."

Wednesday came and as I was about to give my testimony about hell, Josh the minister told me this was the biggest crowd he had ever seen on a Wednesday night for praise and worship service. There looked to be close to 3,000 in the church, which was the total capacity, and over 500 in the two overflow rooms.

He then said, "Spike, they are here to hear your testimony about hell."

When I went and looked out, I noticed the huge crowd. I could feel the look on my face as I said to my wife, "Me – a big old tough guy is scared."

Grace noticed the look on my face. She came over and said, "Spike, don't you worry about the big crowd. You have a chance to save hundreds of people from going to hell with your testimony."

Then Josh told me, "It's time."

Josh went out and introduced me to the crowd. When I was on my way out, everyone stared at me because of all of my tattoos and piercings.

I started off by saying, "My name is not Spike. Spike was the name I was given by the motorcycle gang l was in. My real name is Paul, so just call me Paul. I never want to have anything to do with the name Spike again, except for when l am giving my testimony."

I then went on to tell them how I met Grace. "My wife and l were looking for a Christian store to buy a Bible. I had never read a Bible in my whole life. I had never been to church before. While we were in the book store, we met a lady named Grace. She invited my wife and l to come to her church. Before we left, Grace gave us some Bible verses to look up. She gave us her phone number to help us understand what we were reading. I told Grace everything about me. I am going to tell you the same thing."

Spike's Testimony

"This is the testimony of my life and that hell is real. I was in a motorcycle gang for 15 years. I was in and out of jail. I was stabbed many times. I had been taking drugs for years, when l OD'd for the third time. At the time I OD'd, I was so wasted that I fell out of a two-story window and died. I could see my body lying on the ground. I could see gang members all around me. I could even see my girlfriend at the time, now my wife, crying over me in her arms. I could see myself getting further and further away from my body.
The next thing I knew, l was going into a dark tunnel. I could not see any light. The further l went into the tunnel, the darker it got. When l got to the bottom of the tunnel, it was pitch dark. It was so hot that my skin was burning. I could not see a thing. As l looked around, l could see flames in a far distance. I even heard crying and screaming in the flames.

God is the God of Second Chances

I heard voices in the flames saying, 'Please God, please forgive me. Please God, please help me. Please God, please give me a drop of water. Please God, please get me out of here. Please God!'

The next thing I knew, I saw three creatures in a distance coming towards me. I could only see their red eyes. They were 20 feet tall! So, I did what everybody else was doing here in hell – I prayed! I said what they were saying. The three creatures were still coming towards me. They were getting closer and closer to me.

Then I remembered when I was a little boy, my grandma used to sing a song to me, over and over. It went like this:

> Jesus loves me, this I know
> For the Bible tells me so

I kept singing that song over and over, hoping God would hear me. I even promised God that if he would get me out of there, I would quit the gang and become a minister. After I said that, the creatures were six feet away. They were reaching for me to throw me into the fire.

I said, 'Please God. Please give me a second chance.'

The next thing I knew, I was jolted back into my body by the paramedics. God gave me a second chance.

After God let me come back from hell, I went through eight months of intense therapy in the hospital. I had a broken back, six ribs, my hip, and my right ankle. When they released me, I had eight more weeks of therapy. I promised God when He sent me back that I would quit the gang and study to be a minister for gang members. God answered my prayers. He gave me a second chance and I am here tonight giving you my testimony.

I would like to thank Grace, the minister's daughter, for helping us to learn how to read the Bible. Grace gave us Bible verses to look up. I had never read a Bible in my whole life. I had never ever been to a church. Grace told us to read the Gospel of John. She told us if we didn't understand what we were reading to just call her. Grace was the only one in the store that was not scared to come up to talk to us. Thank you, Grace, you are a Godsend."

When I was done, Josh came out and said, "Paul and Darlene are going to give their life to Christ. They are going to say the sinner's prayer and accept Jesus into their heart as their Lord and Savior. I would like to invite you to come up and give your life to Christ tonight too."

As the crowd was coming up, Josh told me this was the most people he had ever seen come up for an altar call and to accept Jesus as their Lord and Savior. There were over 2,500 people that came to give their life to Christ.

Being born again is God's best free gift that He will ever give to you. All you have to do is repent and accept Jesus into your heart.

Pastor Josh said he will tutor me to get me ready for the seminary in two months.

These are the Bible verses that Grace gave us to look up.

John 3:16
Romans 5:8
Romans 3:25
Ephesians 2:8
Romans 10:13
1 John 2: 1 - 2
Psalm 103:12
Romans 11: 13
Hebrews 4: 16

God is the God of Second Chances.

Chapter 7 – Connor

Why Do Bad Things Happen to Good People?

My name is Connor. I am 17 years old. When I finish high school, I will be going to a seminary to be a minister. I am in the youth group at our church. My mom's name is Brittany. She's in charge of the Bible school at our church. My dad's name is Paul. He's a deacon at our church.

One Sunday night, my mom and dad were talking. I overheard my mom telling my dad that she felt a lump in her breast. She told him she was going to call the doctor in the morning to schedule an appointment.

When she called Dr. Andrew, he told her to come that day, not to wait. My mom left for her appointment. They did a biopsy and a mammogram. After her test was done, the doctor came out and told her not to go anywhere. A few minutes later, they called her to the back. The doctor told her that the biopsy showed that it was cancer. He told her it went into the lymph nodes and the mammogram came back as Stage 3 breast cancer.

"You have to have surgery as soon as possible," Dr. Andrew said, "I can do the
Surgery this Wednesday at 7:00 a.m., two days from now."

We prayed day and night.

When my mom heard the results of her tests, she didn't even blink an eye. She had a positive attitude. My mom would not blame God for her cancer. Her faith never wavered for one second with the bad news. My mom still faithfully read her Bible.

My mom said, "Connor, I am not scared of dying. You don't have to worry about me. I need you to be strong for your dad, Connor. Your dad is going to need you when I am gone. His faith in God is going to waver and will be tested."

My mom told me, "Me and your dad have prayed every day that we would die together. We started praying the day we got married that we would die together."

But, God had other plans.

I told her, "Mom, I promise you that I will take care of dad."

My mom and dad went to the same school and were in the same class since the fifth grade. When they graduated high school, they got married.

My dad would always say to my mom, "I love you, my princess."

Everybody says that my mom and dad's love for each other was a match made in heaven.

When Wednesday came, my dad took off work to be with my mom. She had her surgery and the doctor came out and told my dad the surgery went well. He told him that they removed all the cancer that they could see. He told my dad that my mom would have some pain.

When the doctor released my mom from the hospital, my dad took care of my mom day and night for six weeks. My mom took chemotherapy every Tuesday. My dad took off every Tuesday to be with her. My mom would get sick after her chemo for days. After eight treatments, the doctor ordered more tests to be done on my mom and told us he would call us the next day when the results came in.

God is the God of Second Chances

We prayed day and night that my mom would get good results. The next day, the doctor called. He told my mom, "I have bad news from the tests we did. It showed that the cancer is terminal and that it went into your organs. There is nothing we can do for you."

He then told her, "You have only three months to live. You need to get your affairs in order."

My mom told the doctor, "I will stop chemo so l can spend the remaining time l have left with my family."

The doctor replied, "I can't guarantee you will live for three months without the chemo."

My mom said, "I understand," and she stopped chemo.

My mom said, "Conner, your dad's birthday three months from now. I bought your dad a Bible for his birthday, and l have a letter inside. I want you to give it to him. I will not be here for your dad's birthday. This is where l put it."

Six weeks after my mom stopped her chemo, she passed away. After the death of my mom, my dad was not the same. He was devastated and broken-hearted, and could not control his grief.

I remembered what my mom said. My mom and dad were married for 20 years. My mom was only 38 years old.

My dad was never the same after the death of my mom. The death of my mom caused my dad to rethink his relationship with God. My dad started blaming God for the death of my mom. My mom and dad prayed every day that they would die at the same time.

My dad was so mad at God, he did not even want to have my mom's funeral at any church. But when my mom knew she was dying, she made arrangements at the church where they got married and where she was in charge of Bible school for 12 years. My dad was not happy about having my mom's funeral in church.

He reluctantly said, "Ok, but this will be my last time going to church."

I prayed to God and said, "Please, God, forgive my dad for blaming you for my mom's death. Please God, don't hold my dad responsible for anything he might say when he gets up to talk at the funeral. My dad is very depressed about the loss of my mom."

My dad was the last one to talk at the funeral. He got up as he was walking towards the podium. He passed my mom's coffin and said "l love you, my princess."

You could see my dad was crying a lot. When he started talking, my dad looked up to heaven and said:

"God, l am very angry at You. You took the love of my life away from me too soon. She was only 38 years old. God, You did not give us a chance to live life together. I will never understand You, God. I thought You, God, were a loving God. But You, God, ripped my heart right out of me, l feel so empty on the inside. My God, l am starting to have doubts in You. God, I can't believe such a loving God would cause my wife to get cancer and die. I prayed that You, God, would heal my wife, but You did not. We even had thousands of people praying for my wife day and night. But You, God, would not heal my wife.

My wife was loved by everybody. We prayed every day since we got married that we would die at the same time together. But You, God, would not answer our prayers. My wife would never blame you, God, for her cancer, but l do. I told You, God, that l will never set foot in any church again after my wife's funeral. I have resigned from being a deacon at our church. Conner and l were there when my wife was suffering until her last breath. Even though my wife suffered, she died with her Bible opened to her favorite Bible verse: John 3:16."

God is the God of Second Chances

When my dad finished talking nobody said a word to him.

On his way back to his seat, my dad passed by my mom's casket. He stopped and went up to her and said "I love you, my princess" and gave her a kiss. Then he started crying and went back to his seat.

As the wake was coming to an end, they closed my mom's casket. The pallbearers carried my mom's casket down the aisle. My dad started crying when they passed him and put my mom's casket into the hearse. He rode to the cemetery in the hearse, and I drove my mom's car.

When we got to the cemetery, we said some prayers, and then they lowered my mom's coffin into the ground. My dad really lost it – he started crying uncontrollably. He was so devastated and brokenhearted. My dad was not the same after the death of my mom. He still blamed God for what happened to her. After the funeral, my dad did not say a word to anybody – not even to me on the way home. When we pulled into the driveway, he went straight to his room and shut and locked the door without saying a word.

I was so worried about my dad. It had been three weeks since the funeral, and that was the last time I saw my dad. When I was home, my dad would not come out of his room. When I walked past my dad's door, I could hear him crying. I did not dare knock on his door. He had been crying since the funeral.

I was so worried about my dad that I went to my room and closed the door. I grabbed my Bible and got on my knees, and asked God, "Please God. Please help me help my dad. I don't know what to do. Please God. Help me bring my dad back to you. Please tell me what to do. Please God, give me a sign."

After I prayed, my hand opened the Bible and it landed on the Gospel of John, the third chapter, which has John 3:16. This had to be a sign that God was going to help me bring my dad back to him, even after all the things he said. It must be a sign from God!

As I was reading the rest of the chapter, the Holy Spirit talked to me. Through the Holy Scriptures, God told me to put out Bible verses and inspirational notes all over the house where my dad could see them to bring my dad back to God. While I was on my knees, I asked God to please forgive my dad for what he said at the funeral because my dad is still emotional and broken-hearted.

I started putting out the Bible verses first thing in the morning before I went to school.

On Monday, day one, I put out three bible verses and inspirational notes where my dad could see them. Here is what they said:

1. Dad, God is with you in your darkest hour. God will never ever abandon you. I promise you.

2. Mom and dad, your love for each other are deeply rooted in your hearts.

3. Colossians 2:14. He canceled the record of the charges against us and took it away by nailing it to the cross.

4. Dad, God forgives you for what you said at the funeral. Dad, God nailed what you said at the funeral on his Son's cross.

5. Dad, God knows you are mad at him, but He still loves you, even when you don't want to have anything to do with Him.

6. 1 Peter 2:24. He personally carried our sins in his body on the cross so that we can be dead to sin. By his wounds, you are healed.

God is the God of Second Chances

7. 2 Corinthians 12:9. My grace is all you need.

8. Ephesians 2:5. It is by God's grace that you have been saved.

When I came home from school, I did not see any of the Bible verses I put out. I looked in the trash. I did not see any of the Bible verses in the trash. I hoped he was reading them in his room.

On Tuesday, day two, I put out four more Bible verses. I left a note that said, "Dad, these are the Bible verses about how mom lived her life."

1. Galatians 5: 22. The Holy Spirit produces this kind of fruit in our lives: love, joy, peace, patience, kindness, goodness, faithfulness, gentleness, and self-control.

   Dad, that's how mom lived her life.

2. 1 John 3:16. We know what real love is because Jesus gave up his life for you.

   Dad, God knows what's in your heart. God knows you still love Him. Even though you turned your back on him, He did not turn his back on you. God knows you did not mean what you said at the funeral. He still loves you.

3. Romans 5:5. For we know how dearly God loves us because He has given us the Holy Spirit to fill our hearts with his love.

4. 1 John 2:20. The Holy One has given you his Spirit.

Wednesday, day three, was my dad's birthday. I put the Bible out that my mom gave me to give my dad for his birthday. My mom put a letter inside the Bible. It would have been very special if my mom would have been here to give the Bible to my dad.

"Please God," I prayed, "Let this be the day my dad stays out of his room. My dad has been in his room since the funeral. It's been three weeks. I pray that when I get home from school, I will see my dad out of his room and reading the Bible my mom gave to him."

This is the only Bible verse I put out on Wednesday. This is my mom's favorite verse in the whole Bible.

> John 3:16. "For God so loved the world so much that He gave His one and only Son so that everyone who believes in Him will not perish but have eternal life.

When school ended, I couldn't wait to get home. I pulled into the driveway. When I opened the door, I could see my dad sitting at the kitchen table reading the Bible my mom gave him, with the letter in his hand by his heart. You could see he had been crying. When my dad saw me, he got up and came over to me. He started crying and gave me a hug. He said, "I love you, Conner" and gave me a kiss. He kept saying "I am sorry" over and over.

He then said, "I am sorry for embarrassing you at the funeral. Conner, I said things about God that I should not have said. I blamed God for your mother's cancer and death. I was angry and mad at God. I have been angry at God for over three weeks."

Then he said, "Conner, on Monday morning, I asked God to forgive me. On Monday morning, I got on my knees and I asked God to please give me a sign that He forgives me. I read the Bible verses you put out for me. I asked God to please forgive me for what I said at the funeral. I said, 'Please God, please give me a second chance. You are the God of second chances. Please God, don't turn your back on me as I did You. I am sorry, God, for blaming You for my wife getting cancer and dying. I should have known better than to blame you, God. I'm sorry, God, that I spent three weeks in my room being angry at you. Forgive me, God. I am sorry.'"

Then he told me, "I will start going back to our church next Sunday. I talked to pastor Mike and asked if I could have my old job as deacon back. He said yes. We talked for hours. I asked if I could talk to the congregation and apologize to them for what I said at the funeral."

Then my dad told me about how he read the Bible verses all week. He told me this:

"On Monday morning, I left my room at 11:00 a.m. When I walked into the kitchen, I noticed some Bible verses and inspirational notes. I took them to my room and started reading them in my room. I also fasted Monday.

On Tuesday morning, when I left my room and went to the kitchen, I noticed more Bible verses. I took them to my room. I fasted again on Tuesday.

This morning, on my birthday, when I left my room and went into the kitchen, I noticed one Bible verse and a box, all wrapped up. I went over to see what it was. It was from your mom for my birthday. I opened up the box and found a Bible with a letter inside. I read the letter your mom wrote to me. It was a heartfelt letter. I will cherish it and keep it forever. As I was reading the Bible, I read the Gospel of John. I fasted today for lunch, but I did not go back into my room.

This is your mom's letter.

> My dearest Paul, you are the love of my life. God gave me the greatest gift – you! Every day is the best day of my life because I spend it with you. I thank God for letting you be part of my life. I cherish every moment we have had together. When God made you, He must have been

thinking of me. Paul, please don't blame God for my cancer. I don't. Paul, one day we will be together again. I hope you like the Bible I gave you for your birthday. Thank you, Paul, for letting me be part of your life.

With all my love,
Brittany, your princess forever

Conner, I started reading my Bible again. I am reading the Bible that your mom gave me for my birthday. I asked God to forgive me and recommitted my life to Christ. I said the sinner's prayer again and accepted Jesus back into my life. Connor, God is a God of second chances. He forgives me for what I said. He gave me a second chance. I love you, Conner."

Then my dad looked up to heaven and said, "I love you, my princess. Thank you, my princess, for the Bible and the beautiful letter. One day, we will be together again in heaven. I love you forever, my princess. You will always be in my heart."

God is the God of Second Chances.

Chapter 8 – Suicide

Does God Still Love Me after I Had an Abortion?

It was Easter morning. While my wife and two girls were getting ready for church, the phone rang. I said, "Hello."

It was a lady on the phone. She was frantic and crying. When I asked her what was wrong, she told me she was going to kill herself.

I said, "Why do you want to kill yourself?"

She said, "I had an abortion."

I said, "Even though you had an abortion, God still loves you and God forgives you."

She said, "I caused enough pain, I am going to end it all now."

I said, "If you kill yourself, think about those who love you – your family and your friends. Killing yourself affects them too, not just you."

My wife noticed the look on my face. It was time to leave for church, so I waved for my wife to go without me. So, they left.

I said to the lady, "My name is John, what's yours?"

She replied, "Stacie."

I said, "Stacie, taking your life is not the answer. God's love and forgiveness for you are the answer."

She said "I don't see how God can still love me and forgive me for what I did."

I said, "It doesn't matter what sins you commit, God still loves you. Stacie, God loves you so much that He nailed all your sins on His Son's cross, even the abortion you had. God did that for you, Stacie. That's how much He loves you."

Then I said, "Stacie, you only have to do one thing – repent and say the sinner's prayer. Accept Jesus in your heart as your Lord and Savior. Stacie, do you want Jesus to forgive you and do you want Jesus to live in your heart?"

"Yes," she said.

Then I said, "Repeat after me, Stacie."

The Sinner's Prayer

"Lord Jesus, I know that I am a sinner. I ask you, Jesus, for the forgiveness of my sins. I believe You died on the cross for my sins and rose from the dead. I turn away from my sins and ask you, Jesus, to come into my heart as my Lord and Savior. I believe that Jesus is the Son of the Living God. I believe in my heart that you, Lord God, raised Jesus from the dead. Lord Jesus, take full control of my life from this moment on. I ask this in Jesus' name, amen."

Then I said to Stacie, "Now that you said the sinner's prayer and accepted Jesus into your heart as your Lord and Savior, God will never again remember your sins, even the abortion you had. Now that Jesus is in your heart, you are on your way to heaven."

She said, "I feel like a new person on the inside."

God is the God of Second Chances

I said, "That's Jesus. When you were saying the sinner's prayer, that was Jesus knocking at the door of your heart. And when you accepted Jesus into your heart as your Lord and Savior, that was Jesus coming into your heart, where He will live forever."

Then I asked her, "Where are you staying?"

She said, "I am in a homeless shelter in Houston. I don't like it here. I am scared to leave my room because they have drug addicts, alcoholics, and homeless people staying here. I am so scared to leave my room that they even put my food by the door."

"What about your family?" I asked.

She said, "My mom is taking drugs and my dad OD'd and died a year ago. My mom is still taking drugs. I don't know if she's dead or alive."

"Why don't you stay with us at our house?" I asked.

She said, "I would be glad to."

I then said, "What's the address of where you are staying now? When we get there, I will knock on your door and say my name. We should be there around 1:30. We see you then. Goodbye."

Five minutes later, my wife and kids came home from church. When my wife asked me how the girl on the phone was, I told her she was doing ok and how I talked her out of killing herself.

I said, "Her name is Stacie. I need to tell you something. I hope you will understand what I did. When I was talking to her, she sounded scared and did not know what to do or where to go, so I asked her where she was. She told me she is in a homeless shelter in Houston. She said she is so scared to leave her room that they put her food by the door. She is scared because they have drug addicts, alcoholics, and homeless people staying there. I told her she can stay with us. We need to leave right now."

My wife said she would get the girls.

I told my wife, "We said the sinner's prayer together. She accepted Jesus into her heart. She was going to kill herself because she had an abortion, but l talked her out of it. She asked God to forgive her. I should have asked you first, but she was scared."

My wife said, "That's ok. I would have done the same thing. We have an extra bedroom upstairs. She can stay as long as she wants."

We left the house at 12:45 p.m. and pulled in the driveway of the shelter 45 minutes later. We went inside. There was a man behind the desk.

I said, "My name is John. I am looking for a girl named Stacie. We are here to pick her up – she's going to be staying with us."

He said "I hope she goes with you. She's in room seven."

My wife said in a low voice, "I am sure glad she's coming with us."

We went and knocked on the door. Stacie said, "Who's there?"

I said, "This is John. We talked on the phone?"

She opened the door and you could see that she been crying a lot. I said, "Hello. This is my wife Lisa and my two daughters, Mary and Terry."

She said, "Glad to meet you." Then she closed the door and left with us. She only had a backpack and a bag with all her belongings.

Stacie said, "I can't wait to leave this place. I don't like it here."

God is the God of Second Chances

Then I told Stacie, "You never have to worry about coming back to this place again. You can stay with us as long as you want."

After that, we left that nasty place and were on our way home. Fifty minutes later, we pulled into our driveway. We opened the door and walked in. My wife showed Stacie the room she would be staying in.

Stacie stayed in there for a while and then came down from her room when my wife said it was supper time. Our two girls came down from their room to eat. We all said grace and then we ate. Stacie said that was the best meal she ever had. My wife thanked her.

After supper, Stacie went back to her room. I looked at my wife and said, "We have a lot of Bibles. Why don't we give Stacie one?"

My wife said, "I know just the one to give her." Then Stacie came down from her room.
My wife said, "Stacie, we would like to give you a Bible to read. It's easy to read, and we put some Bible verses for you to look up."

She said, "Thank you very much."

When the girls finished eating, they went up to their room. Stacie went back up to her room and looked up the Bible verses. My wife said to me, "John, what do you think about having Stacie stay with us until we find out if her mama is still on drugs? If she is, we can see if we can have custody of her until she turns 18."

I told her I would start looking for her mama tomorrow.

My wife said, "If Stacie is going to stay with us, we will need to find a school for her and see if she will go to church with us."

Twenty minutes later, Stacie came down from her room. She told us thank you for the Bible verses. When we asked Stacie if she would like to go to church with us, she told us she would be glad to.

Stacie asked "Do you know the minister well?"

"Yes," I told her.

"Do they have a youth group?" she asked.

Again, I told her "Yes."

Stacie then asked, "Can you ask the minister if I can talk to the youth group, so they won't make the same mistake I made?"

I said, "I will introduce you Sunday. Maybe Wednesday he will let you give your testimony."

Stacie said, "Maybe I can give my testimony to other churches and youth groups."

Then Stacie said, "Mrs. Lisa, Mr. John, I am going to tell you about my past. Let me know if you still want me to stay with you. If not, I will understand. I am telling you what I am going to say when I give my testimony at churches and youth groups in the area."

Stacie's Testimony

"Hello, my name is Stacie. My mom and dad have been taking drugs for years. When I was 15, my dad was laid off from his job and he started talking more drugs until he OD'd and died.

Even after the death of my dad, my mama was still taking drugs. She loved her drugs more than me, so I ran away from home and stayed at a friend's house. I had just turned 16.

One month later, I got pregnant by my boyfriend. I told him that I was pregnant with his baby, but he denied the baby was his. He told me he didn't want to have anything to do with me or the baby and that I was on my own. I was scared I would not be able to take care of my baby on my own. I panicked and did not know what to do, so I went and had an abortion. The family I was staying with at the time told me to leave because of my abortion.

I was on my own and had nowhere to go. I could not go home to my mama because she was still on drugs, so I went to a homeless shelter in Houston. I was there for a week. They had drug addicts and alcoholics staying there. I was so scared to leave my room that they would put my food by the door. I got to a point where I did not want to live anymore. Even though it's Easter, I was going to end it all this morning because I couldn't live with the guilt and grief I have.

I have been crying uncontrollably all morning and night for days. One minute, I wanted to kill myself and the next minute I didn't. I couldn't get the guilt out of my head, but I didn't know what to do. I was having second thoughts so I looked around the room for emergency phone numbers for the suicide hotline. I found it in a drawer.

When I called the suicide hotline, a man answered the phone. I told him I had an abortion and that I was going to kill myself, but he talked me out of it. I thought I was talking to somebody at the suicide hotline, but instead I was talking to a man named John. John saved my life. I was one number off of the suicide hotline.

John was my angel that morning that God sent me. Even though it was Easter, the whole family came to the shelter so I could spend Easter with them. Then they asked me if I would like to stay with them. I said yes!

Mr. John saved my life. Now I am a Christian because of him. I said the sinner's prayer and accepted Jesus into my heart as my Lord and Savior. Even though I had an abortion, God still loves me and He forgives me. God loves you just as much as He loves me. God is the God of second chances.

You can say the same sinner's prayer I said. Just repeat after me."

When Stacie finished, my wife gave her a hug and then kissed her. She then put her arm around her and said, "I think you will help more people than you think. You have a very powerful testimony about how you turned your life around. You are an example of God's grace, love, and mercy."

My wife then said to Stacie, "Would you like for John to see if he can find your mama for you and see if she's ok?"

"Please find out for me," Stacie said. "I would like to know if she is still taking drugs."

My wife said, "Stacie, John's a lawyer. He knows a lot of people that can help find your mama."

Then I said, "I am going to start looking for your mama tomorrow and I will let you know when I find out anything."

Four days later, someone called me and said, "We found Stacie's mama. She's in a nursing home. She suffered a bad stroke and can't communicate with anybody. She just stares at the wall and doesn't know anybody."

When I asked my wife to tell Stacie, she said "Ok, I will tell her. I will talk to you later."

When Stacie came down from her room, my wife said, "I need to tell you something, Stacie. John found your mama."

Stacie looked excited, and my wife continued, "I hope you understand what I am about to tell you. Stacie, John said your mama had a bad stroke. She's in a nursing home, but she can't communicate with anybody. She just stares at the wall and doesn't know anybody. Do you still want John to take you to see your mama?

God is the God of Second Chances

Stacie said, "Yes, I want to see her."

When I came home, I took Stacie to the nursing home. When we got there, I said, "If we can't find your mama, we will ask someone."

When they walked in the door to the nursing home, Stacie spotted her mama sitting in a wheelchair in the corner, staring at the wall. Stacie went up to her mama and looked into her face and said, "Hello mama, it's me, Stacie. I love you, mama, I am sorry for running away. Please forgive me. I am so sorry."

Tears were coming down Stacie's eyes. She continued, "Mama, I should have stayed home to take care of you, but instead, I ran away."

Stacie gave her mama a hug and a kiss and said, "I love you mama."

Her mama's face was drooping because of her stroke. As her mama lifted her face, you could see a tear coming down from her eye. Her mama tried to talk, but she could not say anything.

"Mama, I love you," Stacie continued. "I am staying with a really nice family. I will try to come every day to see you. I love you mama. I will see you tomorrow."

As they left, I said, "Stacie, I will take you to see your mama anytime you want."

"Thank you, Mr. John," Stacie said.

Then I said, "Don't blame yourself for what happened to your mama. There was nothing anybody could have done for her. She's in God's hands. Only prayers can help her at this point."

When Stacie and I got home, we sat down in the living room. My wife and I asked Stacie what she thought about us adopting her into our family. Stacie was so excited that she started crying. She told us she would love to be part of our family.

My wife said to Stacie, "Always remember this. Your mama will always be your mama. We just want you to have a place that you can call home. We never want you to have to worry about having a place to stay. We will never let you be homeless again. We love you and we welcome you to our family."

Stacie continued to cry and she said, "Thank you very much."

Stacie then told us she would like to go back to school and get her high school diploma. She told us she wants to go to college and get a degree as a social worker so she can help other teens to not make the same mistake she did.

She said, "Thank you very much, Mr. John, for saving my life, I would not be here today if it was not for you. Thank you again. Love you all."

God is the God of Second Chances.

God is the God of Second Chances

Do you have thoughts of suicide?
Trust in Jesus, He loves you.

Are there any sins in your life you wish you would have never committed? Do you feel like you can never be forgiven for what you did? Are you at a point in your life where you want to end it all?

Don't give up! There is someone that still loves you and forgives you. It's Jesus! Jesus loves you no matter what you did in life. Don't have doubts about God's forgiveness. God loves you so much that He sent His son Jesus to die on the cross for all your sins, even the thoughts of suicide you are having. Give God every sin you ever committed so He can nail all of them on his Son's cross. He will never again remember them.

Do you remember when you were going through the most difficult times in your life, and you felt like Jesus was nowhere to be seen? All you have to do is just look down on the ground – when you only see one set of sandals, fear not! That's Jesus carrying you in His arms through your most difficult times in life, even your thoughts of suicide.

Read God's Holy scriptures when you are having these thoughts. Jesus will never, ever turn his back on you. Lay all the problems you have at the feet of Jesus. Jesus will take care of everything you are going through in life. Trust in Him. Believe in Him. Have faith in Him. Jesus knows what's best for you. He loves you. He forgives you. Remember, God's love for you is agape love.

The Suicide Hotline is 1-800-273-8255. It is open 24 hours a day, 7 days a week.

Glennon Jeffries

God is the God of Second Chances.

Chapter 9 – Your Name Verse

When God Wrote the Bible, He Had You in Mind

God has personally written the Bible for you. God let you be there in person. As you read the Holy Scriptures, you can put your name in place of thousands of Bible verses.

Learn to personalize every word of the Holy Scriptures. Put your name in just a few
Bible verses. His Word was written for you and to you. You are an important part of His plans. Be transformed by the renewing of your mind. Each verse of Scripture in the Bible is for you personally.

These Bible verses are from different Bible translations, not just one. Put your name in the blanks below as you read the Scripture.

NKJV
Psalms 23. The Lord is _____ shepherd; _____ shall not want. He makes _____ to lie down in green pastures; He leads _____ beside the still waters. He restores _____ soul; He leads _____ in the paths of righteousness for His name's sake. Yea, though _____ walk through the valley of the shadow of death, _____ will fear no evil; for you are with _____; your rod and your staff, they comfort _____. You prepared a table for _____ in the presence of _____ enemies; You anoint _____ head with oil; _____ cup runs over. Surely goodness and mercy shall follow _____ all the days of _____ life, and _____ will dwell in the house of the Lord forever.

Psalm 103:12. He has removed _____ sins as far from _____ as the East is from the West.

Isaiah 53:5. But He was wounded for _____ transgressions. He was bruised for _____ iniquities; and by His stripes, _____ are healed.

John 3:16. For God loved the world so much that He gave His one and only Son, so that _____ who believes in Him will not perish but have eternal life.

1 Peter 2:24. He personally carried _____ sins in His body on the cross so that _____ can be dead to sin. By his wounds, _____ are healed.

Romans 8:34. Christ Jesus died for _____ and was raised to life for _____ and He is sitting in the place of honor at God' right hand pleading for _____.

1 Corinthians 5:7. Christ, our Passover Lamb has been a sacrifice for _____.

Romans 5:8. God showed His great love for _____ by sending Christ to die for _____ while he was still a sinner.

Ephesians 3:17. Christ will make his home in _____ heart.

Romans 3:22. _____ are made right with God by _____ faith in Jesus Christ.

ESV
John 1:29. Behold, the Lamb of God, who takes away the sin of _____.

God is the God of Second Chances

KJV
Romans 3:23. For _____ have sinned and fall short of the glory of God.

Romans 10:13. For _____ who calls on the name of the Lord shall be saved.

John 3:3. I tell _____ the truth, unless _____ are born again, _____ cannot see the Kingdom of God.

Romans 10:9. If _____ confess with _____ mouth that Jesus is Lord and believe in _____ heart that God raised Him from the dead, _____ will be saved.

GNT
John 6:37. I will never turn away _____ who comes to me.

1 John 4:9. God showed how much He loved _____ by sending his One and Only Son into the world so that _____ might have eternal life through Him.

1 John 4:10. This is real love not that _____ loved God, but that He loved _____ and sent his son as a sacrifice to take away _____ sins.

Acts 16:30-31. What must _____ do to be saved? Believe in the Lord Jesus and _____ will be saved.

John 3:14-15. The Son of Man must be lifted up, so that _____ who believes in Him will have eternal life.

Psalm 139:13. You made all the delicate inner parts of _____ body and knit _____ together in _____ mother's womb.

Isaiah 30:18. So the Lord must wait for _____ to come to Him so He can show

_____ His love and compassion.

Romans 8:38. And _____ am convinced that nothing can ever separate _____ from God's love. Neither death nor life, neither angels nor demons, neither _____ fears for today nor _____ worries about tomorrow, not even the power of hell can separate _____ from God's love.

5-Finger Bible Verses

These are 5-finger Bible verses. Say your name first, and then read the 5-finger Bible verse.

_____ The Lord is my shepherd. _____ Jesus I trust in you.

_____ Behold the Lamb of God. _____ My sheep hear my voice.

_____ Because He first loved us. _____ To God be the glory.

_____ The disciple whom Jesus loved. _____ The Lord is with you.

_____ Never will I leave you. _____ The Word was with God.

_____ I am with you always. _____ Do whatever He tells you.

_____ Jesus has mercy on me. _____ To whom shall we go?

_____ Father, Son and Holy Spirit. _____ You did it for me.

God is the God of Second Chances.

Chapter 10 – Your Gospel Tract

How Do You Know God Loves You?

John 3:16

Look at the cross

Romans 5:8. God showed His great love for us by sending Christ to die for us while we were still sinners.

God is a loving God and a forgiving God. He loves you and He forgives you. You only have to ask God one time to forgive you for the sins you have committed and you will be forgiven. You don't have to keep confessing the same sin over and over.

Don't have doubts. Trust in God. It doesn't matter how many times you commit the same sin, God still loves you. There is forgiveness – it's Jesus Christ, God's one and only son.

God's love for you is so great that he nailed all your sins on his Son's cross. God did that for you. Only you can make that decision, no one else. It's up to you to accept Jesus into your heart.

Put your name in the blanks in the verses below. Then you will see how much God loves you.

Glennon Jeffries

NIV
Romans 3:23. For _____ have sinned and fall short of the glory of God.

John. 3:16. For God loved the world so much that He gave his One and Only Son, so that _____ who believes in Him will not perish but have eternal life.

Romans 10:13. For _____ who calls on the name of the Lord will be saved.

God sent His Son Jesus as our kinsman-redeemer, He became our sacrificial Lamb. _____ are redeemed through Jesus' precious blood.

ESV
John 1:29. Behold the Lamb of God who takes away the sins of _____.

The Prayer of Surrender

Heavenly Father, have mercy on me a sinner. I believe that Jesus Christ is the Son of the living God and that He died on the cross so that I may have forgiveness for my sins and have eternal life. I believe in my heart that You, Lord God, raised Jesus from the dead. Please, Lord Jesus, forgive me and come into my heart as my personal Lord and Savior. I pray this in Jesus' name, amen.

Revelation 3:20. Look! I stand at the door and knock. If _____ hear my voice and open the door, I will come in.

1 Corinthians 3:6. I planted the seed in _____ heart, and _____ watered it, but it was God who made it grow.

Ephesians 2:8. God saved _____ by grace when _____ believed.

2 Corinthians 5:17. _____ who belongs to Christ has become a new person. The old life is gone; a new life has begun!

Once you repent of your sins and accept Jesus into your heart as your Lord and Savior, He will never again remember your sins.

Hebrew 8:12. I will never again remember _____ sins.

Psalm 103:12. He has removed _____ sins as far from as the east is from the west.

God's love for you is much greater than any sins that you will ever commit in your life.

Romans 8:34. Christ Jesus died for _____ and was raised to life for _____, and He is sitting in the place of honor at God's right hand, pleading for _____.

Jesus is pleading for our sins before the father in heaven.

Even though you repented and accepted Jesus into your heart as your Lord and Savior, you are going to sin. We were born into sin and we all will die a sinner – even Billy Graham, Pope John Paul II, Mother Teresa, and you and me. We all are going to be judged. Being good and doing good for others will not get you to heaven. You can't earn your way to heaven. It's a free gift from God when you accept Jesus into your heart as your Lord and Savior. Repent and say the sinner's prayer above.

Please remember this. If you only have one week to live, will you be ready to face the consequences of what you did in life? Nobody is promised tomorrow. You don't know when you will breathe your last breath. Repent now, before it's too late.

Jesus is God's love revealed.

God's love for you is agape love. ❤

God speaks the loudest when you open the Bible.

The great sign of God's love for us is the sign of the cross.

Jesus is the Way, the Truth, and the Life.

Read the Bible. Remember: The B.I.B.L.E. stands for **B**asic **I**nformation **B**efore **L**eaving **E**arth.

Read the Bible. Read the Gospel of John. Salvation is yours.

God is the God of Second Chances.

God is the God of Second Chances